A Reply to the Question-if it should ever be asked-"Where and what is Bitteswell?" [With plates.]

Anonymous

The BiblioLife Network

GUIDE TO FOLD-OUTS, MAPS and OVERSIZED IMAGES

In an online database, page images do not need to conform to the size restrictions found in a printed book. When converting these images back into a printed bound book, the page sizes are standardized in ways that maintain the detail of the original. For large images, such as fold-out maps, the original page image is split into two or more pages.

Guidelines used to determine the split of oversize pages:

• Some images are split vertically; large images require vertical and horizontal splits.
• For horizontal splits, the content is split left to right.
• For vertical splits, the content is split from top to bottom.
• For both vertical and horizontal splits, the image is processed from top left to bottom right.

BITTESWELL.

A

REPLY

TO THE

QUESTION

(IF IT SHOULD EVER BE ASKED)

"WHERE AND WHAT

IS

BITTESWELL?"

LUTTERWORTH:

PRINTED BY ELIZABETH BOTTRILL AND SON,

1848.

THE REPLY.

THE Village of BITTESWELL has no pretensions to celebrity. It has not been distinguished by the birth or achievements of men of renown, or by the occurrence of remarkable events. Till within a few years, however, in addition to other common modes of travelling, it enjoyed the convenience and comfort of a heavy Chester coach, and was still more enlivened by the shrill notes of the horn of a mail-coach running through, on this the shortest way from London to Holyhead. The passing traveller, if awake, might sometimes enquire its name; or, since so useful a regulation has been pretty generally adopted, might without even *so* much exertion of his curiosity, *read* the

name affixed to the gable-end of a cottage. But
that amazing progress of science, characteristic of
the age, which by the invention of Railways has
suddenly raised so many places, hitherto hidden
in obscurity, to public notice, and reduced so
many which were famous to their original insigni-
ficance, has deprived Bitteswell of what little fame
it may have once possessed as a thoroughfare on
this great road from the metropolis to Holyhead
and Chester. This Memoir, then, does not aspire
to claim any *general* interest, but is intended only
for very limited perusal; being undertaken only
because circumstances have of late years conspired
very much to increase its *local* interest.

EXTRACTS

From the History and Antiquities

of

Guthlaxton Hundred,

in the

County of Leicester,

by

JOHN NICHOLS, F.S.A., Lond., Edinb. and Perth.

"BITTESWELL,

in antient records, is written in various ways.
The first syllables of the word seem to record the
name of some antient proprietor of the place, and
the termination denotes at least the advantage of
good water, if not the presence of some spring of
more especial note.   Our ancestors of old time,
when they became possessed of estates near
springs, or WELLS esteemed for their purity, or for
their mineral properties, and *real*, or as was very
commonly believed, *miraculous* efficacy in the cure
of diseases,—on which account they were often
dedicated to some patron saint,—themselves some-

times assumed the names of such springs or WELLS, and transmitted the adopted name to their posterity

"The greatest part of the parish was antiently the inheritance of the Earls of Leicester.

"The family of FEILDING, progenitors of the present EARL OF DENBIGH, (who were seated in the neighbouring town of Lutterworth) had possessions here many centuries ago, as noticed in a deed of 1192.

"The EARL OF DENBIGH is Lord of the MANOR.

"In 1630 the parish contained 38 families.

"In 1655 there was collected for the relief of poor Protestants the sum of £1, 7s. 9d.

"BITTESWELL is one mile from LUTTERWORTH, two from ULLESTHORPE, three from CLAYBROOK, six from HIGH-CROSS, where the WATLING-STREET is crossed by the FOSS-ROAD, ten from HINCKLEY, eight from RUGBY, fourteen from MARKET-HARBOROUGH, and thirteen from LEICESTER."

DONATIONS.

"1539. March 1. ROBERT DOWSE, Chaplain, made a grant of land for the repairs of the Church

"By a memorandum in the Parish Register, it appears that RICHARD CRANE formerly left thirty pounds to the Poor of Bitteswell for ever; the Principal to be kept entire, and the Interest to be given to the Poor.

"1688. ELIZABETH, widow of RICHARD LORD, of this town, paid the further sum of five pounds into the hands of George Castell, vicar, and John Duell and Richard Gilbeard, churchwardens, as a gift of CHARITY to the Poor of this place.

"1787. In an Act passed for dividing and enclosing several open and common fields and commonable places in Bitteswell, containing 1700 acres, BASIL, EARL of DENBIGH and DESMOND, is described as Lord of the Manor:—the MASTER and WARDENS of the company of HABERDASHERS, in London, as seised of THE RECTORY impropriate, and entitled to all Tithes of Corn and Grain annually arising from the said open and common fields:—as PATRONS also of the VICARAGE:—The Rev. CHARLES JAMES HITCHCOCK, as VICAR, entitled to the small Tithes arising therefrom;—and Holled Smith, Esq. John Goodacre, Gent. Henry Duell, John Lord, John Hirton Garle, and divers other persons, as entitled to the residue of the said open and common fields.

"The Surplice Fees, Easter Offerings and Mortuaries are reserved to the Vicar.

"The PARISH REGISTER commences in 1558; and thence to 1599 is in one regular hand, evidently transcribed from older records.

" By return to Parliament in 1801, it appears that the POPULATION then consisted of 69 families; 192 males and 206 females, total 398, dwelling in 68 houses. Of these 153 were employed chiefly in agriculture, and 141 in trade, manufactures, or handicraft. This return shews that the number of families was nearly doubled since 1630."

Previous to the inclosure of Lutterworth in 1790 and of Bitteswell in 1788, the approach from the former to the latter, by a bad road, and without a

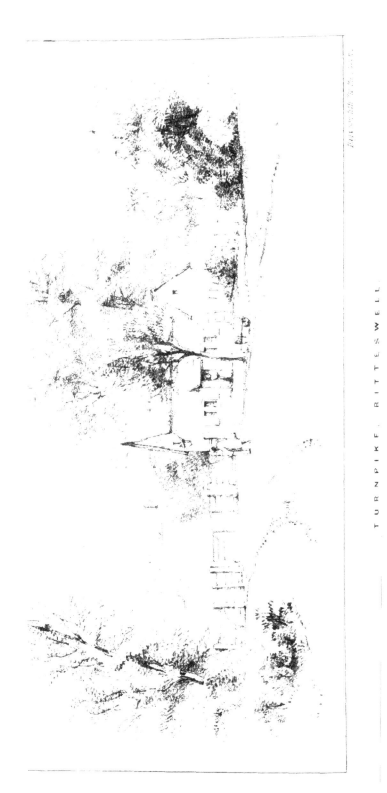

TURNPIKE, RITTESWELL

foot-path, was bleak and rough. This bare and shelterless aspect of the country has been completely changed. The road may now challenge comparison with any; and humble pedestrians, moving in their respective vocations, or walking for health or pleasure, are now indulged with the rural luxury of a well-kept raised foot-path. Altogether, since the village has become well wooded with hedge-row timber and plantations,—intermixed with roofs and gables of houses, barns and cottages scattered amongst them,—the spire in the midst peering over all, the approach is extremely pleasing.

On the left, near the turnpike, is an entrance to the grounds of Thomas Watson, Esq. These premises were formerly the property of Holled Smith, Esq.

The Turnpike is well placed at an angle of the road for the watchful eye of the *careful* and trusty guardian of the Tolls, whose *care* it is that nobody passes without paying his levy. Independently of the propriety of its situation, this token of civilization will not be a disagreeable object to those travellers who do not grudge to pay a few pence for the ease and safety of their own bones, as well as to diminish the toil of those poor animals who are doomed to drag their loads along.

.. And, no doubt, if SHAKSPEAR say truly, that

" Nature teaches beasts to know their friends,"

the poor beasts are very much obliged to all who contribute in any way to lessen their drudgery.

As soon as the Turnpike is passed there is a level brick BRIDGE, over a stream so small as to be easily crossed without observation. Its utmost boast can be that, joining the SWIFT, it is one of the many tributary streams of the AVON of the immortal Bard, which running through Warwickshire, Worcestershire, having passed in its winding course by RUGBY, KENILWORTH, STRATFORD and EVESHAM, falls into the SEVERN at TEWKESBURY.

On the right hand is the gate leading to the home closes of the Vicarage.

A few yards further on, by the hedge side is a small spring, guarded at the sides by stone slabs, and arched over. It has been conjectured that from this spring, or WELL, the village may have derived part of its name.

On the left is the handsome residence of Thomas Watson, Esq.; who at the same time that he built the house, recently much enlarged, laid out the grounds with taste in the modern style.

The next objects which present themselves are

The PARSONAGE and the CHURCH.

The Parsonage is a plain substantial square brick building of the old sort, which, without any external ostentation, has long proved itself adapted to every purpose of domestic comfort and generous hospitality. In 1789 the Offices were added, wall fences were built, and the Garden was enlarged, and laid out, by the new Vicar. From this time may be dated those various and extensive improvements, on all sides, which have contributed to render Bitteswell the pleasant and social place of residence it now is.

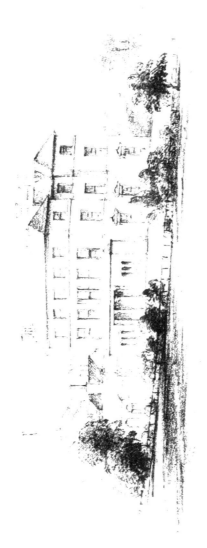

THE RESIDENCE OF THO' WATSON ESQ'

THE VICARAGE, BITTESWELL

BITTESWELL CHURCH.

The VICARS and PATRONS.

——— Jordan, ...1220 ⎞
William Chaplain, ..1238 ⎟ *Abbot and Convent of*
Robert Dowse, ...1534 ⎟ *St. Mary de Pratis,*
John Handcock, died 1562 ⎠ *at Leicester.*

Richard Tilley, ...1563   *Thomas Croft.*

Edward Duckmaster, 1606 ⎱ *Henry Dillingham,*
                        ⎰ *of Cotesbach.*

Blasius Adam, living 1631 ⎞
Elisha Bourne, ...1632 ⎟ *The Company of*
George Castell, ...1660 ⎠ *Haberdashers.*

Samuel Nicholson, ..1704 ⎱ *Edward Shaw, pro*
                       ⎰ *istá vice.*

Isaac Crewe, ...1717 ⎱ *Governors of Christ's*
                       ⎰ *Hospital.*

William Stanton, ...1757 ⎞
James C. Hitchcock, 1762 ⎟ *The Company of*
James Powell, ...1789 ⎟ *Haberdashers,*
George Monnington,..1844 ⎠ *London.*

The late Vicar, whose memory will always be dear to those who survive him, was born in London, educated at Harrow School, admitted at Clare Hall, Cambridge, where he took his degrees of A.B. and A.M., and instituted in 1789 to this vicarage.

The following inscriptions are upon his tomb in
the churchyard, on the north side of the chancel.

TO THE MEMORY OF

THE REVEREND JAMES POWELL, M.A.,

DURING 55 YEARS

THE RESIDENT VICAR AND FAITHFUL PASTOR

OF THIS PARISH.

AFTER OFFICIATING AT THE MORNING SERVICE

WITH UNDIMINISHED ENERGY

HE DIED SUDDENLY IN THE EVENING OF

SUNDAY THE 21st DAY OF APRIL 1844

IN THE 80th YEAR OF HIS AGE.

. . . . . .

AND OF MARY HIS WIFE

DAUGHTER OF

MR. TWINING OF LONDON.

SHE DIED THE 13th OF JANUARY 1794

IN THE 24th YEAR OF HER AGE.

BITTESWELL.

THE CHURCH

"is dedicated to St. Mary. It is an antient structure, and consists of a very strong and tall embattled tower, crowned with a low spire. The interior has only a nave and a chancel. In the base of the tower, on the south side, is a large arch. hollowed in, to about the depth of three feet, and originally about seven feet high in the crown. The vault or circumflexed ceiling of this cavity is in panelled stonework, not ill-handled, and the back composed of square ashlers, well jointed. It appears to have been made at the time the steeple was built. As the figure of it greatly resembles the mural arches which we frequently see in church walls, over the figures of bishops, knights, and other eminent men of past ages, it is not unreasonable to suppose that this arch is the receptacle of some deceased man of note, or benefactor to the church.

"Within the tower hang four small bells, round which is inscribed

"HENRY PENN, he made me, 1706.

"WILLIAM TALBOT and WILLIAM CRISPE,
Churchwardens.

"The tower is also furnished with a good clock, placed here at the expence of Mrs. ANNA MARIA SANDERSON, relict of the Rev. THOMAS SANDERSON.

"The Church of Bitteswell was given to the Abbot and CONVENT of LEICESTER, by Robert de Arraby, and was afterwards appropriated to that Abbey.

"In the matriculus of 1220 it is described to be under the patronage of the abbot; the vicar Jordan having been instituted by Hugh bishop of Lincoln.

"In pope Nicholas's valuation, 1290, this church is rated at £5, 6s. 8d., and the vicarage at £2.

"In 1344 the procurations were 7s. $6\frac{1}{4}$; the vicarage was rated at 8 marks, and paid 2s. for Peter-pence.

"In 1534 the value of the vicarage was £3, 6s.

"This impropriation, says Mr. Baxter in 1622, was lately the inheritance of Mr. Dillingham, of

Cotesbach. It is now purchased by that worthy
company of Haberdashers in London, in 1632, and
by them restored to the church again. Part
the fund arose from the generous benefaction
Dame MARY WELD, relict of Sir JOHN WELD,
wealthy citizen of London."

The benefaction of ROBERT DOWSE in 1539 having been long applied to other purposes than the
repairs of the church, the Rev. JAMES POWELL ef-
fected the restoration of the fund in future to its
original destination. The lands (32 acres) were let
at an improved rent of £96. per annum. He ad-
vanced the sum required, and proceeded immedi-
ately to restore the sacred edifice. The lands are
at this time let at £60. per annum.

1812. The church was NEW-ROOFED in the inter-
val between the 27th of April and the 5th of July.

1822. Between the 7th of April and the 11th of
August all the old PEWS were removed, and much
accommodation gained in the new seats. The

tables of the COMMANDMENTS and the COMMUNION rails were also renewed.

1842. The TOWER of the Church was thoroughly repaired.

In a memoir of this kind, the merit of a humble, but clever and industrious artist, should not be passed over without a record. The whole of the carved work was executed by Mr. W. BROUGHTON of this place, when a very young man.

1842. The CHANCEL was decorated with a new WINDOW. This, with the painted glass, whose rich but soft and subdued tints, correspond so well with the solemn offices administered beneath its mellow light, was given by Mrs. ANN TWINING.

1844. A barrel ORGAN had been presented by the vicar. This was now replaced, agreeably to his directions, by the present excellent finger-organ

In 1847, the Rev. GEORGE MONNINGTON, the new

vicar, always active, and devoted to the duties of his ministry, exerted himself with success in procuring an extension of the churchyard on the north side. The consecration of the new ground was performed on the 20th day of July, by Dr. Davys, the bishop of the diocese, in the presence of numerous clergymen and a large portion of the parishioners.

Though neither the exterior nor interior of the CHURCH may offer much to excite the admiration of the architect or antiquary, yet the old and simple character of its outline, its good proportions, its churchyard and blue slate tombstones, which, owing to the elevation of the ground, are open to view, its row of fine old sycamore trees,—not to omit the clock on the steeple,—all these together—so prominent in the middle of the village, with sufficient space around to be seen to advantage all at once,—form with the adjoining Parsonage a most pleasing combination ;—from which, had we no more practical evidence, we should draw the favorable conclusion that both rich and poor know the value of time,—that they appreciate the blessings of a true faith, and are zealous and regular in their attendance on public worship.

Adjoining the garden of the Parsonage on the north side, is a modern house, built in 1834 by the then vicar, as the future residence of his daughter. The first occupier was Mrs. ANN TWINING, from TWICKENHAM in Middlesex. When the decease of Mr. Powell obliged Miss POWELL to relinquish the paternal roof under which she had hitherto passed her happy days, and to seek a new home,—she had not far to seek it, nor had any difficulty in finding it,—but was welcomed by her aunt to that retreat which had been prepared for her by her affectionate father,—to their mutual comfort and happiness.

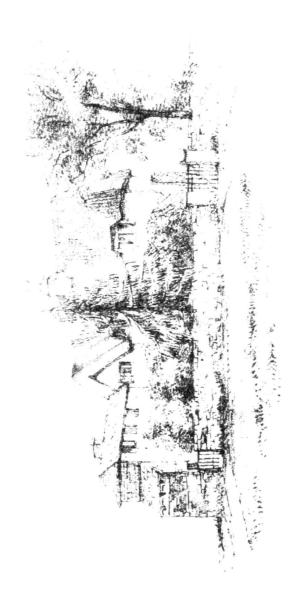

THE RESIDENCE OF M⁻ TILT.

THE RESIDENCE OF MRS. CALDECOTT.

From a sketch by Mrs. Caldecott.

BITTESWELL HOUSE.

On the Green a turning to the left leads to a house built in 1800 by Thomas Grace Smith, Esq. and since became the property of the late John Sherard Coleman, Esq. It is now inhabited by Mrs. Caldecott, daughter of the late Rev. Dr. Marriott, of Cotesbach, and widow of Abraham Caldecott, Esq. of The Lodge, Rugby. This house commands a cheerful prospect over the green fields, with the pinnacled tower of Lutterworth Church in the distance.

BITTESWELL HALL.

The turning to the right on the Green leads into the turnpike road from Lutterworth to Leicester, passing in front of this spacious mansion, erected in 1838 by the late WILLIAM CORBET SMITH, Esq., and now occupied by ROBERT FELLOWES Esq., of SHOTTESHAM, in the county of NORFOLK.

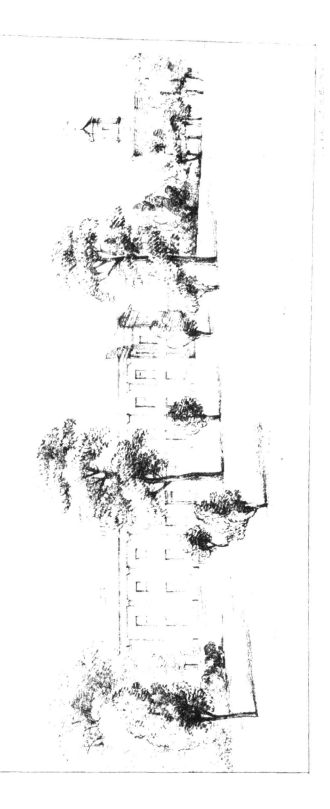

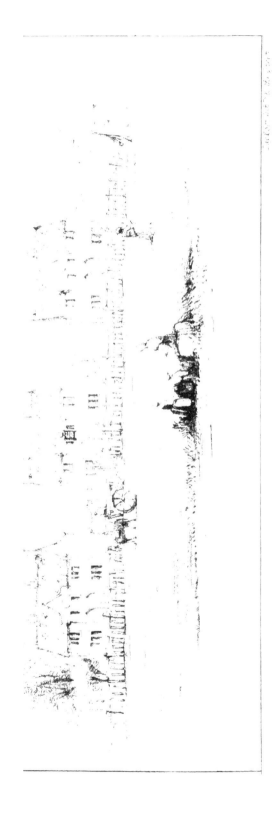

THE ALMSHOUSES.

There stood on the Green, till lately, a row of miserable old mud cottages or huts. The site having been kindly granted by Lord DENBIGH, the lord of the manor, not only was the unsightly nuisance removed, but a handsome row of ALMS-HOUSES, after a design by WILLIAM PARSONS, Esq., Architect, was substituted in its place by Miss POWELL, in accordance with the wishes of her aunt. Over the door of the centre building is the following inscription.

1847.

These Almshouses
were built from funds left for
Charitable purposes by the late
WAKELIN WELCH, Esq.
of Camden Place, Bath, and
ELIZABETH his Wife,
Sister of the late
Rev. JAMES POWELL,
Vicar of this Parish.

The first persons admitted to the benefit of this Charity, are Elizabeth Broughton, Richard and Elizabeth Burrows, William Sutton, Dennis and Hannah Angrave, Mary Williams and Ann Kind, John and Catherine Bailey.

THE NATIONAL SCHOOL.

A little further on is the NATIONAL SCHOOL-ROOM
and Master's house, with this inscription. :—

This SCHOOL
for sound Religious Education
was begun
by the Rev. JAMES POWELL,
Vicar of this Parish,
and
Completed and Endowed
by his DAUGHTER,
in the year 1844.

O let me have understanding in the way of GODLINESS.
Psalm ci. 2.

At the extremity of the village a lane straight on
leads to the GLEBE FARM.

At the distance of a mile the turnpike road
enters the parish of CLAYBROOK, of which ULLES-
THORPE, at the distance of another mile, is a ham-
let. Having crossed a bridge over the railway
and turned to the left, we arrive at the ULLES-
THORPE STATION, ninety miles and three quarters
from London. Between this station and Lutterworth there is a constant communication, as well
by social and indiscriminating OMNIBUS, as by
genteeler and more exclusive FLY.

SCHOOL, RITTESWEIL.

Lightning Source UK Ltd.
Milton Keynes UK
UKOW07f1857301115

263854UK00009B/278/P